AT THE Aquarium

FANTASTIC FISH

by
Mignonne Gunasekara

BEARPORT PUBLISHING

Minneapolis, Minnesota

PHOTO CREDITS

All images are courtesy of Shutterstock.com, unless otherwise specified. With thanks to Getty Images, Thinkstock Photo and iStockphoto. Plant Vectors Throughout – Baksiabat, MicroOne. Front Cover – Beth Swanson, Elena_sg80, Rich Carey. 4–5 – Vlad61. 6–7 – Bass Supakit, EdBrown, iarecottonstudio. 8–9 – magnusdeepbelow, Martin Prochazkacz, Rich Carey. 10–11 – ChooChin, Pakhnyushchy, Rich Carey. 12–13 – Vladimir Wrangel, Kletr, SergeUWPhoto, unterwegs. 14–15 – Daniel Huebner, katatonia82, Agami Photo Agency, Choksawatdikorn, VikiVector. 16–17 – Sascha Janson, Christopher Moswitzer, Sascha Janson, Jens Petersen/Wikimedia Commons. 18–19 – Kris Wiktor, divedog, Ian D M Robertson. 20–21 – Krzysztof Bargiel, magnusdeepbelow, Neelkai Photography, acro_phuket, KPaulina. 22–23 – Katy Foster, stockfour, calimedia, Ryan Janssens.

Library of Congress Cataloging-in-Publication Data is available at www.loc.gov or upon request from the publisher.

ISBN: 978-1-64747-404-1 (hardcover)
ISBN: 978-1-64747-411-9 (paperback)
ISBN: 978-1-64747-418-8 (ebook)

For more information, write to Bearport Publishing, 5357 Penn Avenue South, Minneapolis, MN 55419.
Printed in the United States of America.

CONTENTS

WELCOME TO THE AQUARIUM!

Welcome to the aquarium. Aquariums look after sea animals. Many aquariums do lots of work to protect wild animals, too.

Let's look at some fantastic fish. They come in many sizes, shapes, and colors.

Dive in to learn about eight kinds of fish.

PYGMY SEAHORSE

A pygmy seahorse is only about 1 inch (3 cm) long.

Pygmy seahorses are tiny. They live on **coral** in warm, **shallow** waters.

The seahorse uses its tail to hold onto coral. The female seahorse leaves her eggs in the male seahorse's **pouch.**

Seahorses are different from other animals because the males carry the young.

Pygmy seahorses blend in with the coral they live on.

GIANT MANTA RAY

Giant manta rays usually live alone, but they come together to eat.

The giant manta ray is the biggest kind of ray. It can grow to over 26 feet (8 m) wide!

Giant manta rays have the largest brain of any fish. They are very smart.

These fish have good memories.

The rays can recognize themselves in a mirror.

RED LIONFISH

Red lionfish live in reefs in warm waters. Their fins have **venom**-filled spines.

The venom in the spines helps protect these fish from **predators**.

Sharks, eels, and other big fish eat red lionfish.

Red lionfish don't have many predators where they live in the Atlantic Ocean.

COMMON CLOWNFISH

Clownfish live in anemones.

Clownfish are also known as anemonefish because they live in anemones.

Clownfish and anemones help each other. Anemones sting clownfish predators. Clownfish clean anemones.

Clownfish are covered in a slime that protects them from stings.

An anemone

FLYING FISH

Flying fish can grow up to 1.5 feet (45 cm) long.

There are around 40 types of flying fish. They can be found in warm waters all over the world.

Flying fish can't actually fly. They swim underwater to build up speed. Then, they jump into the air and spread their fins.

Flying fish mainly eat small animals and plants called **plankton**.

Flying fish glide. They don't fly.

STRIATED FROGFISH

This fish is also known as the striped anglerfish.

Striated frogfish can be found in reefs. They also live on or near the bottom of the sea.

This fish sits still and gets **prey** to come to it with a body part that looks like a tasty worm.

When the prey is near, the fish quickly sucks the meal into its big mouth.

This fish can swallow prey that is almost twice its size.

LEAFY SEA DRAGON

Leafy sea dragons look as if they are covered in leaves. This makes them harder for predators to spot.

Leafy sea dragons live around seagrass, seaweed, and rocky reefs.

The male sea dragon looks after the eggs. He carries them under his tail.

Leafy sea dragons eat tiny creatures such as plankton.

SPOTTED PORCUPINEFISH

Spotted porcupinefish live near caves and on reefs.

Spotted porcupinefish can be found in warm waters around the world. They have strong jaws and sharp, spiky spines on their bodies.

A porcupinefish can suck water in through its mouth. This makes its body puff up and its spines stick out.

Spotted porcupinefish eat snails, sea urchins, and crabs.

Porcupinefish puff up to protect themselves from predators.

THANKS FOR VISITING!

Thank you for stopping by the aquarium. If you like fantastic fish, there are things you can do to keep them safe.

People fish too much of many types of fish.

Fishing too much can hurt fish and their ocean homes. Buying and eating fish caught through **sustainable** fishing is one thing we can do to help.

Sustainable fishing makes sure there are enough fish left in the sea for the future.

Check food labels for symbols like this.

GLOSSARY

coral a group of rocklike structures made from the skeletons of sea animals also called coral

plankton tiny animals and plants that float together in water

pouch a body part made for carrying babies

predators animals that hunt other animals for food

prey an animal that is hunted and eaten by another animal

shallow not deep

sustainable done in a way that does not use up everything there is

venom a harmful substance that is injected through a bite or a sting

INDEX